THIS IS WHAT HAPPENS NEXT

Also by Daniel MacIvor:

# THIS IS
# WHAT
# HAPPENS
# NEXT
## BY
# DANIEL
# MacIVOR

**PLAYWRIGHTS CANADA PRESS**

TORONTO

For professional or amateur production rights, please contact:

The Gary Goddard Agency
149 Church Street, 2nd Floor
Toronto, ON M5B 1Y4
416-928-0299, meaghan@garygoddardagency.com

LIBRARY AND ARCHIVES CANADA CATALOGUING IN PUBLICATION
MacIvor, Daniel, 1962-, author
        This is what happens next / Daniel MacIvor.

A play.
Issued in print and electronic formats.
ISBN 978-1-77091-200-7 (pbk.).--ISBN 978-1-77091-201-4 (pdf).--
ISBN 978-1-77091-202-1 (epub)

        I. Title.

PS8575.I86T45 2014          C812'.54          C2013-908485-1
                                              C2013-908486-X

We acknowledge the financial support of the Canada Council for the Arts, the Ontario Arts Council (OAC)—an agency of the Government of Ontario, which last year funded 1,681 individual artists and 1,125 organizations in 216 communities across Ontario for a total of $52.8 million—the Ontario Media Development Corporation, and the Government of Canada through the Canada Book Fund for our publishing activities.

 Canada Council Conseil des arts
for the Arts  du Canada

 ONTARIO ARTS COUNCIL
CONSEIL DES ARTS DE L'ONTARIO
50 YEARS OF ONTARIO GOVERNMENT SUPPORT OF THE ARTS
50 ANS DE SOUTIEN DU GOUVERNEMENT DE L'ONTARIO AUX ARTS

 Canada

 Ontario
Ontario Media Development
Corporation

FOR BILL W. AND HIS FRIENDS

*This Is What Happens Next* was first produced by Necessary Angel Theatre Company and the Canadian Stage Company in April 2010 at the Berkeley Street Theatre. It featured the following cast and creative team:

Performed by Daniel MacIvor
Directed and dramaturged by Daniel Brooks
Lighting design by Kimberly Purtell
Sound design by Richard Feren

## CHARACTERS

ME

WILL

WARREN

SUSAN

AARON

MIKE

KEVIN

*On stage left is a chair, a pair of shoes beside the chair, a coat stand with a suit jacket hanging on it. On stage right a small table with a shelf below where a glass and a vodka bottle sit. These furniture pieces are placed near the edges of the playing space.*

*ME enters the theatre through the audience wearing street clothes (a pink shirt). He carries a book and a venti Starbucks coffee. He makes his way toward the stage. The house lights remain up.*

**ME**

I'm sorry I'm late, I'm sorry I'm late, I'm sorry I'm late, I'm sorry I'm late, I'm sorry I'm late. That's the first thing I say when I enter any room. I'm always late. Chronically late. Terminally late. And I'm really trying not to be late these days. I'm really trying not to be late because when I'm late I get annoyed and when I'm annoyed I get resentful and… well I don't even want to think about where resentment gets me. Resentment is fatal.

But here I am late. But it wasn't my fault. That must be the slowest Starbucks in the city. In the country. And I've been around. Twenty minutes for a decaf grande soy latte? And this is not even a grande, it's a venti—and we won't even bother getting in to how that happened. Regardless I'm late. But it's not my fault. It was these two women. I'm walking to the door of the Starbucks and there are these two women behind me chatting away and I think, "I'll be the nice guy," and I hold the door for them. And this is also a little annoying. I don't need a thank you but a head nod might be nice. An acknowledgement of my existence. How hard is a head nod? How hard is that. I should probably be on the stage. I'll go on the stage now.

> *ME steps onto the stage. During the following he changes from his street shoes to the shoes that have been sitting near the chair. At one point he considers putting on the suit jacket but forgoes it, thinking it's too formal. As he continues the house lights fade.*

So I know the deal. I let them in ahead of me and that means that they're ahead of me and of course they order eight lattes. Eight? Don't you have to call ahead for an order of that size? *(re: book)* This isn't a Bible, by the way, it's *The Story of Philosophy* by William Durant. It's pretty good; I'm trying to expand my mind. What's left of it.

> *He puts the book on the shelf near the vodka.*

So I'm waiting. And so far I'm not overly annoyed. I get to order my decaf grande soy latte but of course there's an eight latte backup so it's going to be a while. But lucky for me the first two are made and the women are chatting away and sipping on them and one says to the other, "I can't taste my flavour. Can you taste your flavour?" And the other one says, "No but I wasn't going to say anything." So the first woman says to the barrista guy making the latte's, "Did you put the flavor shots in?" He says, "Yep." She says, "Well I don't taste anything." And the guy says, "I'll make you new ones." What? Just like that? And he turns to me and says, "You're not in a rush are you?" Well actually I am. Clearly. But when he asks me "You're not in a rush are you?" I don't say anything because I don't want to sound annoyed. I just turn away and think about being late and try not to be annoyed. But then I realize not saying anything when he says "You're not in a rush are you?" is a very annoyed thing to do, it's downright rude. So I turn back to say something but the moment has passed and it's too late to say anything. And so now I'm not only failing at not being annoyed I'm failing at hiding that I'm annoyed. So now I'm just officially waiting and annoyed. Meanwhile there's this other barista guy who's making some kind of flavoured latte concoction in a big vat and he's squirting all this syrup into the vat with this squirty bottle thing and he's counting the squirts under his breath, "Twenty-four, twenty-five, twenty-six," and in an effort to take my mind off being annoyed I start counting the squirts along with him in my head, "Twenty-seven, twenty-eight, twenty-nine," and then he stops he asks the other barista guy,

"How many squirts all together?" And the guy calls back, "Forty-six. Then the squirting guy goes back to squirting where he stopped squirting and he's standing there kind of looking lost holding the squirty bottle of syrup stuff over the vat and it's clear he can't remember where he left off counting before he stopped to ask how many total squirts. But I remember! "Twenty-seven, twenty-eight, twenty-nine." So I call out, helpfully, "Thirty," but he doesn't hear me so I call out again, kind of annoyed, "Thirty!" And now I think he's just blatantly ignoring me because the whole place can hear me, and there's quite a lineup now, and of course they just think I'm this crazy annoyed guy yelling out random numbers. And the squirty guy starts squirting again and counting, "Forty, forty-one, forty-two." So no wonder nobody can taste their flavours they're ten shots off! Reason to be annoyed! Or, not really. But I am trying to change! I am. Really. Trying. Trying to be less easily annoyed. Trying to be less trying. Trying to be different. Trying to better myself. In lots of ways... I'm reading philosophy. Trying to change my attitude. And this is where we're supposed to start.

*A moment.*

Snow.

*A moment.* ME *looks to the booth.*

Oh. Isn't...? Wasn't...?

Really?

Fine.

I thought something was supposed to happen there. It doesn't matter. It would have been over the top anyway. Forget it.

So, snow. Snow is a perfect way for me to illustrate one of my major issues. I find snow terribly annoying. And I know I'm a bit of a blamer. I blame those two women for being late. I blame snow for my shitty winter. I get it. And so I decided I'm going to change my attitude and I decide to start with snow. Because I see snow and I think: "Snow, oh great, shovelling and cold feet and icy roads." So I'm trying to change that. But you see for someone like me it's not about changing shovelling and cold feet and icy roads into something positive and saying, "Snow: oh great, sleigh rides and roasted chestnuts and tobogganing." Because someone like me can turn those things into negatives justlikethat. I can so easily make it: sleigh rides: think of the horses; roasted chestnuts: taste like barf; tobogganing: there's a broken hip right there. No for me I have to go to the original negatives shovelling, cold feet, icy roads and transform those, so it becomes: shovelling: good outdoor exercise; cold feet: new boots; icy roads: that's a tough one but I came up with icy roads: a minor fender-bender, a cop comes to take my information, he's handsome and gay and he gives me his number. Like that's going to happen. Maybe in a movie. I might have seen once. And anyway that's a bit triggery for me. I have a thing with people. I'll think of something else for icy roads. But anyway yeah so. Yeah. That's my story.

7

I thought I'd have more to say about that. I had more to say about it when I was in the bathroom working on it earlier. Unfortunately concise for once.

Okay stay in the moment.

I bought these shoes in Montreal. They make nice shoes in Montreal. Well they don't make them there, they import them. They make them in Italy I guess. They're overpriced. But the salesman said they'd bury me in them. Actually he didn't say that. He said they'd last forever. I just thought, "They'll bury me in them." That would be a terrible way to sell shoes. Maybe not for me. For most people. "We've got a shirt in the back we can bury you in that too." Oh, this is a pink shirt. I got it in Berlin years ago when pink was supposed to become the new black. That never caught on unfortunately.

Actually it's not the same shirt. I did get a pink shirt years ago in Berlin when pink was supposed to become the new black. But that shirt wore out. I got this shirt in honour of that shirt. I didn't have to tell you that. You never would have known the difference. But I'm trying to be honest.

It's too bad pink never did become the new black. I was hoping it would. Imagine that. Next time you go to a function look around and imagine everyone in black in pink. It would change the world.

Some people say it's not pink. I say it's deep pink. Someone said it was fuchsia but I think fuchsia has more blue.

Oh by the way, you should turn off your phones because if they light up I get distracted and slooooooow down, and if I get distracted and slow down we'll be here forever. So for your sake I'd turn off your phone. *(takes out his phone to make sure it's on)* I'm leaving mine on though. I'm expecting a call. From my lawyer. I wish I was kidding. It's been a shitty couple of years. But I don't want to get into that. Or... Argh.

Why is this so difficult? I'm not asking you. It's a rhetorical question. Well it's not rhetorical, I can answer it. This is difficult because I had publicly stated that I wasn't going to do this kind of thing anymore. And I didn't want to do this kind of thing anymore because to do this kind of thing you have to have a story and I've been trying to avoid stories. Telling stories, making up stories. See what I had wanted to do was have a real life and tell the truth and stay in the moment, and to do whatever I could in the moment by moment to secure myself a happy ending. I'm all about the happy endings now. So I tried that. It didn't work out. So here I am. So I planned to just tell the truth. But what's the truth anyway? It's true to me. But to really tell the real story we'd have to have all the... players... everyone involved. Telling their truth. Not just me. "He'd" have to be here. And my lawyer probably. My father, why not. Bring on my astrologer too. All the victims of my behaviour. The ghosts of the victims of what might have happened. And we don't want that to happen. So now I need a story. And that's difficult because part of what I've been trying to do is stay in the present, in the now, in the "this" as it were—but a story isn't interested in the this, a story is all about the "next" and then the next and then the next next and ultimately there's an ending. And my endings have usually been anything but happy. And also this is difficult because in order to tell a story I'd need to use my Will to do that. And lately I've been trying to avoid my Will. I mean clearly it's available to me, I'm here. But my Will is a pretty single-minded, sarcastic, self-centred kind of guy. And I'm trying not to be that guy. Will can turn me into a bit of a monster. An angry giant crushing everything in his path. It's not pretty. And also my Will doesn't believe in happy endings. But without Will there's just… this. And we've done the Starbucks, we've done the snow, we've done the shoes and the shirt and the cellphone. I don't think this is going to be enough.

All I really wanted was to see you smile. All I wanted to was hear you laugh. I just wanted to give you a happy ending. But something has to happen so…

*Suspenseful music.*

Here we go.
There is a story. I'm sure you're relieved to hear that. And the story is about Kevin, or well, it's not really about Kevin but Kevin

is central. He's a kid. He's seven. Or eight. No... or. He's seven! Kevin represents the inner child. And I guess me as a kid. And there's Kevin's father Mike. Who is kind of like my father. And me. Partly me too. It's all about me I guess. And there's Kevin's mother—Mike's ex-wife—but I don't think we get to meet her though but she's important in the story. And there's Kevin's Uncle Aaron. He used to be Kevin's Aunt Erin. He changed it from Erin with an E to Aaron with an A when he had his gender reassignment surgery. Well not the whole thing. He still has his, or she still has his... It's confusing. Anyway Aaron represents my sexuality and my issues with gender and that's confusing.

*In the distance we hear giant footsteps approaching. Growing louder and louder.*

And also there's a giant. Kevin tells the story of a giant. In a fairy tale he makes up. The giant is a metaphor for... Or a representation of... Oh we don't need to get into all that. Look, it will all be okay. It'll be okay. You'll get what you came for. You'll have something to talk about. Something will happen. Something will definitely happen. Just whatever you do don't get too close, don't mention philosophy and for God's sake don't let him have a drink!

*We hear a terrible sound.*

*Blackout.*

*Light shift. Music: "Happy Ending."*

*WILL walks into the light, wearing the suit jacket.*

**WILL**

Hi. I'm back. Sorry about that meandering, "spontaneous" opening. What was that all about, with the Starbucks cup and the recent experiences and the nervous charm and *The Story of Philosophy*? Eek. That old chestnut. That's a big part of the problem. It's a cute book. Concise. Covers a lot of ground. A little bit of information about a whole lot of things. But for someone like Me a little bit of information can be a very dangerous thing. It's an okay book, all the regulars: Hegel. Voltaire. And of course you've got your Schopenhauer. Don't get me started on Schopenhauer. We can just break out the razor blades now. For those of you who know Schopenhauer, you know what I'm talking about, and for those of you who don't, count yourselves lucky. Hey listen. This music? Have a listen. It's called "Happy Ending." Doesn't it just make you want to... Makes you happy. Well, it's been quite a couple of years for Me. Got married. Fell into a dark abyss of cocaine and alcohol addiction. Lots of unhealthy sexual behaviour. In and out of recovery. Filed for divorced. Lost the house. Lost thousands and thousands of dollars. Alienated people who loved Me. Disappointed a whole gazebo full of family and friends. And on top of it all aging badly. Well no wonder, it's been quite a couple of years. But when I say all that with this playing doesn't it sound so much better? No, not really. Because "Happy Ending" is just the name of a song. When the song is over you're not happy anymore. When the song is over the song is over. And that's because there's no such thing as a happy ending. I mean sure that's arguable. You've got, what, *The Little Mermaid*. But no, because the real ending is she doesn't get the prince, she gets her tongue cut out and she turns into seafoam; the rest of that story is just Disney. And there's what, something real... John Denver and all that uplifting Colorado "Rocky Mountain High" stuff. No, because the real story is he forgets to put gas in his plane and they find his foot floating in the ocean, the rest of that story is just a made-for-TV movie. Or maybe... something big... "God"? Ah, but that just seems like more Disney to me. No, if we're going to talk about endings we'll have to talk about polar bears and drinking water and hurricanes and terrorism and the decline of Western civilization, or let's just cut to the chase: Y'all die. Thank you and good night, I'll be here all week, tell your friends. No. Forget about the ending, there's no happy in the ending. You want to be happy. I'm assuming that. So what are you going to do, sit around and wait for your happy ending? You might as well just stay home and watch TV or go shopping. It's not going to happen. There's only one way to be happy. And that is to know what you want and use your Will to get it.

Okay so, apparently there needs to be a story. And apparently that's become my job. Well that's easy. Just tell the truth. All you have to do is adjust some facts, alter some names, change a sex, make some substitutions: like hot tub for waterbed, that kind of thing, and add a "once upon a time." So... Once upon a time there was... Warren. Warren: forty-five, looks it, trim, works at it, gay, comes off mincier than he thinks, a bit of a blamer, but overall not a bad guy. Warren wants something... He wants... He wants to get his stuff back. Bad breakup. Left in a hurry. The ex kept the house. Time has passed. The ex has moved on. Warren's a little pissed. He's got some stuff still at the house he wants. His... sneakers, his windbreaker, a book, his tax stuff, a... a CD... a John Denver CD. Sure let's bring him into the mix. Why not, just because he has bad taste doesn't mean he's not a good person. He's got a weak spot for John Denver, so what. It's his stuff. It's your stuff, Warren. You want your stuff back. This is bullshit. You go and get your stuff.

*WARREN's phone rings.*

And don't answer that phone!

*Light shift.*

**WARREN**
This is bullshit! This is bullshit! Okay. I call him last week and tell him that I want to come and get my stuff today, Saturday, and he says: "Saturday might not be the best day for me." Oh really? Well Saturday is the best day for me. I'm fine. I'm fine. I've got an apartment. I've got a job. I make money. I made the

divorce trip to Ikea for carpets and can openers and tea lights and hangers. I've got parking. I've got a permit. Fifty dollars a month I park on the street no problem. Just outside my place. Around the corner. Past the market. Past the liquor store, the pastry place, the smoke shop, the bookstore and just beside the Italian bistro, it's very convenient. Have the whole driveway now, have the whole thing. Get a couple of junkers and park them in the yard. I'm fine. I'm so fine I'm thinking about taking a tai chi class. How's that okay? I've even been talking to someone about taking private lessons because I'm better one-on-one. Well he would say I suck at one-on-one but let me rephrase that. I'm better one-on-one with SANE people who don't have these arbitrary INSANE rules like: "Don't kiss me like that" or "Always ask me how was my day" or "Come to bed when I say so." That's just… Look, I just want my stuff, okay. My my my my sneakers and my my windbreaker; I'm not going out and buying a new windbreaker when I have a perfectly good windbreaker sitting in my closet. HIS closet. Yeah fine. Have the closet. Have the house. Have the pool I paid for. Yeah yeah he dug the hole, well you know what if nobody PAYS for the POOL all you've got there is a HOLE in the GROUND. Fill it with water, then you've got MUD. But he doesn't have MUD he has a POOL. Enjoy the pool but I want my windbreaker. And my sneakers, they're not just sneakers they're Cole Haan. And that book I was reading, that philosophy book, I'm thinking about taking a class. And my tax stuff. I want my tax stuff. And I don't want my stuff tomorrow I want my tax stuff today. Because today is Saturday which means that tomorrow is Sunday and my week starts on Sunday and I don't want my new start to start next week, I don't want my new start to start in the middle of the week, I want my new start to start tomorrow, which is Sunday so I want my stuff today which is Saturday. Oh but he's having a barbecue today. Oh really? How nice for him. Well I have something to do today too. I'm meeting Susan today. She's my lawyer. And my friend. I'm meeting my friend and lawyer Susan today. So there. Good for me. But I don't want to meet Susan today. And I don't even want to take her phone calls to tell her I don't want to meet today because all Susan will say is don't you go to that barbecue. She told me that as my lawyer. And my friend. "Don't you go to that goddamn barbecue!" A barbecue. How nice for him. Him and all his new himbo friends in their mankinis sipping their Sea Breezes around the pool I paid for. Hey boys enjoy the pool! And don't forget to put plastic sheets down on the new sofa before the piss party. Okay, that was unnecessary. I'm not trying to say I wasn't there, okay. I'm not saying I'm perfect and don't have my flaws. But try living with his stridency. And his opinions. And his repetition. Oh my God. The same stories over and over and over again. Da da da da da da da da da da da Norway da da da da da da da da hot tub da da da da da da leather chaps. And no sense of occasion. No sense of appropriateness. It doesn't matter who's in the room. These are not the people for this story. The sex party story is not for these people. Save the sex party story for the sex party people. The sex party story is not for my mother. My mother doesn't get it the sex party story. I

don't get the sex party story. Well that's not entirely true but...
I just want my stuff. Oh and "Ask me how was my day, ask me
how was my day, why don't you ever ask me how was my day?"
Oh I don't know, maybe because I'm a narcissist and I don't think
of it, okay. Or maybe because I don't need to because you tell
me anyway all he does is complain and complain and complain
and complain and complain and complain and finally one night
I innocently say, innocently I say: "Well why don't you quit your
job." And so he does and I might as well have gotten a tattoo on
my forehead or shot myself in the face because boy oh boy do I
really have to eat that for dinner for the rest of my life. "I should
never have let you make me quit my job." I should never have let
you make me quit my job? You "*let me*" "*make you*" quit your job?
How does that work? What personality type is that, "Victim"
or "Controlling"? My head explodes. No it doesn't. I'm fine. Oh
oh oh oh and "The Chest of Drawers." The Chest of Drawers.
We don't need another chest of drawers we have four chests of
drawers. We've had this conversation, just because there's space
doesn't mean there's room. Nevertheless, one morning I wake
up and I walk into the living room—hungover like a bull in a
G-string—and I look out the window and what's sitting on the
front step? A chest of drawers. Now I don't think that chest of
drawers was walking down the street and decided it wanted to
live with us. I don't think it's a stray. I think somebody told
somebody to drop off that chest of drawers, and that somebody
wasn't me. And we've had this conversation. Just because there's
space doesn't mean there's ROOM. Empty space is doing

something. It's being empty. That's not me being controlling that's me having an aesthetic. And I don't want to have this conversation again so I get in the car and I start driving to Delaware, but I can't find the ferry because I took the wrong road and I don't have my wallet or my passport anyway. And so I go home and he's ironing. And he should never iron because he thinks too much when he's ironing. But I try to reason with him and I say, "You think it's about the Chest of Drawers but it's not about the Chest of Drawers." But all he hears is "You're wrong." And he comes at me, the iron high over his head, knuckles white on the handle. I scream like a girl and run backwards down the stairs and lock myself in the bathroom. After about an hour I come out and he's sorry, you can see that he's sorry, his eyes are full of sorry. But I think yeah well that's the same sorry you're going to see in his eyes in the prisoners dock when he's on trial for my murder. He'll be sorry then too. But we talk it out and make up, as it were, and he decides he's going to go and get some coke. There's a solution! And what about that rule? The rule that when one of us says "I'm going to get some coke" the other one is supposed to say "Maybe you shouldn't." So I try and enact that rule and he says, "I'm going to get some coke," and I say, "Maybe you shouldn't," and he says, "Fuck you." And what does that do but give me licence to fuck him too. And it wasn't just him okay I know I know. I was there. I was part of it too. Some nights I'd get the coke and I'd hide a bit of it away, and we'd do it all and he'd say, "Is there any more," and I'd say, "No it's all gone," and I'd wait until we started to get sketchy then I'd "ta

da!" the stash out and be the hero but then that would be gone—
because at some point it's always going to be gone—and he says,
"There's more isn't there." And I say, "No that's it." And he says,
"No you're hiding some." And I say, "No really it's done it's all
gone." And he says, "Well I'm going to get some more." And I
say, "It's six o'clock in the morning." And he says, "So what?"
And I say, "Okay here's a hundred bucks get two." I was there I
know. But a kitten? A kitten? A kitten? And without a conversation? I'm out of town—making money—and he's on the phone
saying, "Guess what I got?" And I'm hoping it's a urinary tract
infection… But he's not on the phone telling me he's got a urinary tract infection he's telling me he got a kitten. A kitten?
Without a conversation? A kitten is not a plant. You don't just
put it in a pot of dirt and water it. It's a kitten, it might live for
twenty years. I don't feel we've got twenty years left at this point.
I don't feel like we've got two years left at this point. And so no
I'm not over the moon about the kitten. And two days later when
he calls to tell me that the kitten died of leukemia, no I don't
sound upset because I'm not upset because we don't need a kitten
right now. Oh and "I can't do anything right." Well no not if you
keep bringing home kittens. A kitten without a conversation
does not go in the "right" column. I should have listened to
Susan. My lawyer. My friend. She's going to be calling any
minute and tell me not to go to the barbecue. But she's wrong.
She's right but she's wrong. She's right as a lawyer but she's
wrong as a friend. She's not usually wrong as a friend. As a friend
about us she was so right. She said we were a bad match. And I

knew we were a bad match but I'd always had good matches before and they never worked out so I thought a bad match might be just the ticket. I'd learn to be the quiet one, I'd learn to listen, I'd be kinder, gentler. Oh oh oh oh oh oh oh but "come to bed, come to bed, come to bed." The more he'd ask me to come to bed the less I'd come to bed. If you don't stop asking me to come to bed I'm never coming to bed. "Come to bed, come to bed, come to bed, come to bed."

"Come to bed."

"In a minute."

"You said that an hour ago."

"Then this came on."

"What is it?"

"I don't know."

"You don't know what you're watching?"

"It's a movie."

"Hey isn't that guy who's married to Hilary Swank?"

"They're divorced."

"But that's him?"

"Was him."

"He's not dead. Is he dead?"

"No."

"Well it's still him, whoever he is."

"Chad Lowe."

"Right. Chad Lowe. Isn't he—"

"Yes."

"You don't know what I was going to say."

"Yes he's Rob Lowe's brother."

"Oh. Right. I thought so. Come to bed."

"In a minute."

"Chad and Hilary are divorced?"

"Years ago."

"They seemed so happy."

"Not to me."

"Come to bed."

"In a minute."

"Why's he wearing that terrible wig?"

"He's playing John Denver. It's the John Denver story."

"Wow. Everything from Schopenhauer to John Denver."

"What?"

"You like John Denver?"

"No. Yes. Why? I'm indifferent."

"You're indifferent?"

"Yes."

"You'd rather watch a movie about someone you're indifferent to than come to bed with me."

"It's drawn me in."

"Past indifference?"

"I'm curious."

"You're curious about it."

"It's a curious thing."

"The story of John Denver?"

"It's a curious movie."

"Why?"

"Let me watch it and I'll analyze it later."

"DVR it."

"What?"

"DVR it. Or PVR it. Whatever they call it. The thing we pay for."

"*We* pay for."

"What?"

"Just let me watch the movie."

"No. Come to bed."

"Not right now."

"You like Chad Lowe? You're a Chad Lowe fan?"

"I'll be up in a minute."

"He's a wonderful actor Chad Lowe?"

"Leave me alone."

"Leave you alone?"

"Yes."

"Leave you alone?"

"Jesus. Yes."

"Leave. You. Alone."

"Yes."

"Do you not love me?"

"Do I not—?"

"Love me."

"Do I not love you?"

"Yes."

"Yes."

"Yes what?"

"I do."

"Do what?"

"Not love you. Not love you. Not not not love you. I do not love you I cannot stand you. I would rather be anywhere than where you are; I'd rather be dead than where you are. And if it came down to me dead or you dead I'd pick me dead because if you were dead I'd be left alive with the memory of how much I cannot stand and do not love you. Do you have any more questions?"

And yes I like John Denver. So what? No he's not Miles Davis. No he's not Arcade Fire. So what? It's not like I own the oeuvre, okay. I just like a couple of songs. I only have one CD. And that's another thing I want back. I want my John Denver CD and I want it today.

And okay yes maybe I should have come to bed. But if I was going to come to bed I should have done that weeks ago, months ago. Just bit the bullet and came to bed. But it was too late now. But he thought everything was fine. He thought Chad and Hilary were happy? She didn't even thank him when she won an Oscar. You have to thank your husband when you win an Oscar. That's not love. Okay there's the word. Love. Love. I don't even know what that is. What is it? Compromise? Companionship? It sounds like something to be sentenced to: "Twenty years of hard companionship!" Love. I can't find the hook. It's too simple or too complicated. It's like a foreign language everybody's speaking but

I don't understand. It's like a word everybody uses but nobody knows what it really means. Like "presently"! Presently does not mean "now," presently does not mean "currently." Presently means "soon." Presently means "in the near future." Use it in a sentence? Okay. "Presently I will be getting my stuff." "Presently I will be happy I left you." And yes it was me yes I left. And of course I did that badly. But what was I supposed to do? I'm in another city and it's the somethingth of December and we're on the phone and he's asking me if we should get a Christmas tree. And I know. I know at this point.

"Should we get a Christmas tree?"

"Is there a time when we could talk?"

"We can talk now."

"I don't want to live this way anymore."

"Can we climb out of this hole together?"

"No."

"Can we try?"

"I don't want to try."

And yes okay fine it was on the phone but what was I supposed to do? Say yes to the tree and then go home and break up with him in front of the tree and ruin Christmas forever? But now apparently everything's fine. Now he's not crazy anymore. Why did he wait to stop being crazy until we broke up? Now he's happy. Now he's civil. "Today might not be the best day for you to pick up your stuff." How civil. He's happy. Well I don't believe it. His civility is carved to an awfully sharp point; his happiness is a bit too acidic for me. Oh he's having a barbecue? Well you know what? I never liked barbecues. I never owned a barbecue until I met him. Or a microwave. And suddenly we're barbecuing every night for dinner and microwaving the leftovers for lunch. Partying with cavemen and picking up robots online for sex. I don't even remember their names. I don't even remember the sex. Oh but there's a tape! Oh but there's footage! I'm sure that will resurface if I ever decide to run for alderman. But I don't care about that stuff. That's not my stuff. I want my stuff. I want my windbreaker and my sneakers and my book and my tax stuff and my John Denver CD. I want my stuff and I want it today.

*WARREN's cellphone rings again. He takes it out and looks at it.*

**VOICE OF WILL**
Don't answer that.
  Don't answer that.

*WARREN answers the cellphone. Light shift.*

**SUSAN**
*(on phone)* Warren? It's Susan. Are we meeting today or what? Call me back, you idiot. And don't you dare go to that goddamn barbecue.
  *(SUSAN turns off the phone.)* He better not have gone to that goddamn barbecue. And I'm not saying that as Warren's lawyer I'm saying that as Warren's friend. Those two were a bad match.

Like a ferret and a hamster. You ever see a ferret and a hamster
go at it? A bloodbath. My youngest daughter had a hamster and
then she hit puberty and decided that ferrets were cute—there's
a red flag. First it's the ferrets, then it's the piercings, then the
tattooing, then the floor-length capes and the Aleister Crowley.
Then she wants to change her name to Cerridwen and move her
bedroom into the basement. Full moons she's sneaking out to
spend the night with her dishwater-complexion friends at that
swamp behind the soccer field that they call "the heath." You
know what she asked for for Christmas last year? You know
what she asked for for Christmas last year? Fangs! She wanted
to have her incisors filed down to fangs. What happened to
Cabbage Patch Kids? What happened to Barbie Dream Homes?
What happened to Tickle Me Elmo? "No you're not getting fangs
for Christmas." Goddamn vampires. Ah they're all Mormons
anyway. Honest to God. Kids. But she's just the dull throb to
the sharp pain. The sharp pain that would be my oldest daughter. Three years at an American liberal arts college at thirty-five
thousand dollars a year and she quits in her last term to marry a
snake. A snake. Rotten? Rotten? Rotten? He gets her involved in
a real-estate scam. A real-estate scam? In this economic climate?
I can't talk about it it's in the courts. And what can I do? It's not
like I can pull any strings. Twenty-five years at Shmulik Ginsberg
Family Law and I can't pull any strings. I could maybe get you
a caterer cheap, or a limo service, a landscaper. That's about
it. Shmulik Ginsberg. *(She dials on her cell.)* And nobody calls
him Shmulik anyway, everybody calls him Sam. He just likes

"Shmulik" because it takes up more room on the marquee downstairs. *(into phone)* Answer the phone, you moron. *(She hangs up.)*

He better not have gone to that goddamn barbecue. And I told him. I told him when it started. I told him before it started. I told him long ago. I said, "Warren, you do not have the constitution for coupling." Which is true. I call it like I see it. I know people. And you want me to tell you something? It's a very slim margin of humans who do have the constitution for coupling. It's a fifty per cent divorce rate, people. You put that and human nature in a calculator and you know what comes up? Pre-nup. Pre-nup. Pre-nup. And even then. Even getting that. Standard pre-nup. All laid out on the boardroom table. Client comes in with his fiancée. All he's got to do is sign. You can see he feels a little queasy. I hand him the pen. He goes to sign, he stops, he goes to sign, he stops, he looks up at me: "This doesn't feel very good." No it doesn't feel very good, it's not a time-share in Costa Rica it's a pre-nup it's not supposed to *feel good*. But bingo bango Missy sees her way in. She starts digging in her purse. Pulls out this chewed-up plastic pen. Goes to hand it to him: "Here, use my lucky pen." Oh what a gesture. What a woman. Offering the dagger with which he will stab her in the guise of the lucky pen. I can see what's happening here. I can smell it. His heart melts. And I can see in his eyes what he's about to say, "Awww we don't need a pre-nup." So I step in just in time and I say, "Hey hey hey, who needs luck when you've got love?" Thank you very much. That gets us over the hump long enough to get signatures and off they go for cake arranging or flower tasting or whatever the hell they're spending their time and money on. About twenty minutes later I go into the boardroom to clean up and what's on the table? That's right. The lucky pen. And I keep that lucky pen for two months waiting for the frantic "Did I leave my lucky pen there?" phone call. Never comes. Come on, she fished that pen from a junk drawer ten minutes before she left the house. The ruse of the lucky pen. I've seen it all. I'll give her back her lucky pen when she comes in for the divorce. And divorce! Trying to get people through that these days. There's a walk in the park, there's a weekend at the beach. Another client of mine. Gervase. Gervase and Sonja. Oh my God. Gervase. Dumb. Lazy. Rich. There's a stellar combination. And beautiful. Lighter fluid on the fire. Gervase became my client a few years ago when he came into the office all upset about how his psychic just told him the world was going to end in five years, not in eight years like his psychic told him last time, so Gervase wants to adjust his living will accordingly. What? Whatever. Doesn't matter to me, bring on the end, a change is as good as a rest. Then a couple of days after this Gervase goes out and buys a turtle. A turtle? A turtle? This guy thinks we've got five left and he goes out and buys a turtle? Those things live for seventy years or something. That's a scary thought all by itself. Then Gervase meets Sonja. Sonja. Gervase and Sonja are both models. They met in rehab for Ritalin addiction. There's a prescription for bliss. Within a month they're married, fourteen months later we're working on the divorce. A couple of days ago Gervase walks in to my office with a bowl on his head. "Why do

THIS IS WHAT HAPPENS NEXT

you have that bowl on your head, Gervase?" "It's not bowl it's a hat." Models! "Take off the bowl sit down shut up and tell me what you want." And Gervase tells me he wants to withdraw the divorce papers. Again! "Why this time, Gervase?" "Well the other day I dropped by the house to get…" Laid! That's the only reason he's dropping by the house. To get laid. Happens all the time. Familiar sex. It's very dangerous. The lure of familiar sex can hold divorces up for years. Of course sex is scary you just have to watch porn with the sound down to see that. Of course you want to hang your hat on a hook you know. And who wants to subject themselves to the horrors of dating? Come on! True story. Here's me:

"So tell me a little about yourself?"

Here's him:

"Well I'm a very active member of NA because last year I got addicted to marijuana because I was smoking it medicinally to counteract some gastrointestinal issues that I developed as a result of my HIV meds which also gave me anal fissures, they're not malignant but my doctor wants me have them removed before I go back to school this fall to study fashion design."

AT THE AGE OF FIFTY-TWO! It's a circus out there. And now Gervase is in my office telling me that he and Sonja are still in love. Love. Oh please. I don't care how you feel. I'm not a marriage counsellor. You want a marriage counsellor at three hundred dollars an hour? I suggest you get a therapist. It's half the price and twice as indulgent. I don't care how you feel. It's a ledger. A ledger. A ledger. A list of objects and numbers connected to the objects. A chest of drawers? Fine. How much is it worth? Put it on the ledger. I don't care how you feel about the chest of drawers, I don't care if you met buying the chest of drawers, I don't care if your grandmother strapped that chest of drawers to her back and swam all the way from the homeland with it. Just tell me who owns it what it's worth put it on the ledger. Period-osky. *C'est ca. Tout fini. Nada* more.

Gervase says I need a vacation. Yeah, Gervase, I'm taking a vacation this weekend. I'm taking Percocet Airlines up to Gin Lake. Shut up, Gervase. But he's a cutie. He's got that going for him. What's he so upset about divorce for? My marriage ended and I'm fine. Except I got the goddamn kids. No no, they're the best thing that ever happened to me. Or they ruined my life. Who knows. I don't know what might have happened because this happened. But when all is said and done and at the end of the day I'm a good mother. I am. Because I set boundaries without being overbearing. I let them make their own mistakes. I let them have their diversions. Their books. I'm not a fan of books. I read when I have to but I can't say there have been many books I've got through without at some point wanting to chuck them across the goddamn room. And self-help books? Oh my God. Listen, if you're thinking about buying a book called *Should I Leave?* save yourself the $25.99 and leave. And fiction? Meh. I haven't got the imagination for fiction. They made me turn in my imagination when I gave up my expectations. I'll wait for the movie. But I let the girls have their books. The little one has her Aleister Crowley—she doesn't really read it though it's more of a prop. And the older one went through her Candace Bushnell phase. Candace Bushnell. *Sex and the City.* Candace Bushnell, I'd like to burn that bitch in effigy. I tried to watch that TV show, but what the hell was it? Four whores sitting around tables in restaurants stuffing their faces with cheesecake and bread. And what did they weigh? A hundred and twenty pounds collectively. I actually saw it once where the little scrawny one said, "I'm going to drown my sorrows in another piece of cake." Yeah maybe with a bucket beside you. What were they selling besides herpes and bulimia? God I hate that shit. Bring back the Barbies, at least they didn't talk. But I wasn't coming down on my kids about this stuff. Their books, their diversions. I let them make their own mistakes. But the older one I don't know. I think it's just prison for her. A real-estate scam? In this economic climate? She might as well have been stealing wheelchairs from war amps. I mean give me bank robbery, give me hijacking. These days a real-estate scam makes organ harvesting look classy. But the young one, who knows? She's young. The tattoos won't go away but the piercings will grow over. And there are worse things than hanging out in a swamp with a bunch of vampires wearing purity rings drinking Dr. Pepper from a goblet. I indulge her, I call her Cerridwen, and she seems pretty happy in the basement. But I was thinking, one thing I might have done wrong, maybe I should have got her a turtle instead of a ferret. A turtle and a hamster might have got along better. But not really though. It was the hamster was the mean one. Tough! That ferret didn't stand a chance. Ah what difference does it make turtle ferret hamster. We all end up feeding the same field of daisies. Everything ends. Or turns into something else. Or goes away. Just like when you're fifteen years old at the high-school dance and Lionel Richie is singing "Easy Like Sunday Morning," and Elliot Hillman finally asks you to slow dance and introduces you to the concept of engorged for the very first time. But four minutes and sixteen seconds later it's all over and you can never get it back again. And thirty years pass and Elliot Hillman finally comes out of the closet after two marriages and you can't get into the high-school dance without passing through a metal detector and Lionel Richie has a daughter who grows up and becomes famous for being best friends with a skank. That's the way it goes. It ends and it turns into something else. Or it just ends. *(She takes out her cellphone and looks for a number.)* Okay, Warren, that was strike three. And I cancelled a date today to meet with that son of a bitch. Goddamn barbecue. Warren's out, date's back on. Yeah I'm dating. I met him online. Third date today. Nothing's happened yet though. He's shy. He's an astrologer. There's nothing wrong with that. Astrology's no worse than anything else. And I believe in things. I believe in lots of things. What I don't believe in is people. Because I know people.

> She pushes a button as if turning on a CD; it's "Easy" by the
> Commodores.

I'm just gonna chillax with some tunes and see if I can get the reluctant Romeo on the line and rebook the date. Fingers crossed third date we'll get below the belt. "Oh she's randy!"

That's the Commodores. Lionel Richie at his best, baby. A girl can dream can't she? *(into phone)* Hi Aaron, it's Susan. Listen—

*The sound of giant footsteps and a record scratching.*

*Light shift.*

**WILL**

The Commodores? What's next John Denver?

*Music "Happy Ending."*

And she doesn't read? Oh, okay. I guess I can get behind that. And domesticated turtles don't live to be seventy years old, they're lucky to see seven. She'd probably know that if she read. *(He takes a sip from the Starbucks cup; he immediately spits it out.)* Jesus Christ! That's fucking COLD! Grrr. Oh listen, "Happy Ending"! Yay. But as for happy endings I'm sorry to say that if we were to continue telling her story it would not be a happy ending. If she were to continue on the road she's on it will be a ripped-from-the-headlines type ending: "Mother Drugged and Killed in Bathtub by Satan-Worshipping Teenage Daughter." But the good news is the daughter ends up becoming rehabilitated in prison and finds God. Although she does eventually go back

33

to jail for bombing a mosque. You win some you lose some. No happy endings here. Which brings me to Mister Arthur Schopenhauer Fellatalist—urm—Philosopher, who would say that it is the will of the horny lawyer mother, the will of the vampire mosque-bombing daughter, the will of the I'm-going-to-get-my-stuff Warren that leads to their unhappiness. Because Arthur Schopenhauer was the guy who said "A life of will is a life of misery." Oh okay. Well let's take a look at Arthur Schopenhauer's life shall we? Once upon a time Arthur Schopenhauer was born to a privileged, cultured family. But tragically Arthur's father dies when he is very young. And this is tragic because little Arthur has a nasty, nasty relationship with is mother. Arthur Schopenhauer is a very serious kid but his mother is a party girl of the highest order. They're fighting all the time. One night his mother actually pushes little Arthur down a flight of stairs. Pushes him down a flight of stairs! So clearly Arthur Schopenhauer has approval issues. And all he really wants all his life is to be famous. But nobody wants to read all this pessimistic writing he's doing. So he ends up sixty-nine years old living in a dingy little flat in Frankfurt paying people all over Europe to cut out any tiny mention of his name in the paper and send it to him. That's just sad. Maybe if Arthur Schopenhauer realized he could use his Will rather than deny it he would have... I don't know... lightened up a bit... learned how to play the fiddle or something. Change your attitude, Arty. And I'm not talking about some pathetic "from now on I'm going to look at snow as a good thing" attitude. What the hell was that?

No, I say if life gives you lemons—break out the tequila. Make a change, take a stand, tell your story, get your stuff. Of course some people just don't have the balls. *(He finds this hilarious.)* You'll get that later.

*The cellphone rings.*

Oh good! What's next?!

*Light shift.*

**AARON**

*(He moves his hands as if laying out cards.)* This is the recent past. This is the present. This is the near future. Everybody wants the same thing behind the cards. In the past people want hardship and strife. In the present people want searching and solitude. And everybody is looking for one thing behind this card: the Future. Everybody wants change. Everybody wants to feel like they're good people having some bad luck and moving toward something better. They want to hear that everything's going to change. They want the Ace of Pentacles: wealth and health. They want Strength with her hand on the lion's mane. Or the Lovers. We're all looking for the hookup. Even if they're already with someone, maybe there's somebody better out there, the real one, the one who's going to save me. We're all blindfolded sticking our hand in a bag of snakes looking for the eel. That sounds bitter I know. I blame my ex-girlfriend. I blame people

who lie; I blame people who use other people to forward their own agenda; I blame righteous people... I used to be righteous. Until I realized that righteousness is damn ugly when it takes off its choirboy robes. Righteousness has no eyes, no ears, just a big mouth in its oversized head—oversized to hold all those facts, all that information—and huge hands, huge hands for pushing, pushing away anything that doesn't agree. *(He looks at his hands.)* I asked them if they could make my hands bigger. Ever since I was a little girl I hated my little hands. And my long hair. My Gramma, she got it. She didn't care. She was the one who took me for my first haircut at a barber when I was twelve. I had this long curly hair that my mother treated like it was hers and that my father looked at as proof. And I was twelve and sick of my long hair and my little hands and of course my boobs had already started. All the girls praying for boobs and all I wanted were big fleshy hands and short hair. Well I couldn't do anything about the boobs and the hands but my hair I could. And my Gramma got it. She didn't take it personally. And I sat in that barber's chair and when it was over I felt the bristles on the back of my head and it was like the chains had been cut off and I was two feet taller. My parents called me selfish, but I wasn't doing what I wanted, I was doing what I was. My mother doesn't believe God makes mistakes. Yeah well okay but that's the kind of thinking that makes me worry for the kids. For kids like me. For my nephew.

My sister still calls me Erin. I changed it from Erin with an E to Aaron with an A but when my sister says it I can still hear the E. But she chooses me over her ex when she needs someone to look after the kid, but that's because her ex is usually too drunk or hungover to be responsible. So she puts me on the list above a deadbeat chronic alcoholic. That's something I guess. See my nephew, he's at that age where he's still acting from his own truth but he's starting to notice that he's being judged. The looks in the room when he says that at Halloween he wants to go as the Little Mermaid. He loves *The Little Mermaid*. And that doesn't mean anything, he likes giants too. But I want to make sure he grows up in a world that gives him the space to find out if he's a mermaid or a giant. Not in a world that says "you can't be who you are because we don't have a box for that on the form," that says "you can get married but you can kiss my ass," that raises its eyebrows every time he leaves a room. So I guess I want to change the world. How do I do that? I have no idea. But I know it has nothing to do with righteousness. You don't get there by writing letters to the editor and eating indignation for breakfast, puffed up with pride. You see righteousness doesn't like contradiction and we're made of contradiction. Righteousness wants you to choose. Righteousness is my ex-girlfriend. Calling herself an activist and making her speeches about the rights of the marginalized. And when I told her I wanted to transition she was all for it. She was supportive. She was encouraging. And she came to all my appointments and she used me in her speeches and she was at the front of the crowd in every parade. But after I had my breasts removed and the hormones kicked in and I was living as a man I felt more myself than I ever had before. I didn't need a penis to be a man. I didn't need any more operations. I didn't need to manipulate my body any more, I was me now. I was who I am. So I tell her. Oh then everything changes. She doesn't know what her speeches are about anymore. She doesn't know what she's supposed to be fighting for. She doesn't know what story to tell. She doesn't know how to feel. She doesn't know what to call me. Call me contradiction. Call me the future. Call me Aaron. See, righteousness wants the definitive; righteousness wants you to have the operation. Righteousness wants that box checked. So I leave. Fine. This is who I am. This is where I belong. This is my power. This is my place. This is my body. And if that makes you uncomfortable I understand that, because I'm talking from the physical and we're trained not to talk from the physical. We're trained to use our language to tell stories and talk about feelings. But language is physical. Language is made in the body—these bodies we're so afraid of. Our bodies become our nightmares when they should be what set us free. And that is the freedom I want for my nephew. That's how I want to change the world. Will I get there? I don't know. But it's pretty funny that I'm the father figure in his life. I was supposed to babysit him today but I might have a date. I decided to start again. She cancelled but then left a message to say she was suddenly free. Suddenly free. That's a nice feeling. It would be our third date today. I haven't told her yet. I don't know how she'll take it. She's pretty cool. She's a lawyer. She's older. Got a couple of kids. If I see her today I tell her. Who I am. The contradiction. And if she doesn't go for it that's okay. Maybe I can save myself three hundred bucks and get some free legal advice. I'm thinking about suing my ex-girlfriend for being a cunt.

If go on my date the kid goes to Mike's, his father's. Which probably means an afternoon on the dirty floor in front of the TV, building castles with beer caps. The kid means a lot to me. But the Goddess has her plan. I go with the Goddess. Goddess, tell me what to do. *(He moves his hands as if flipping over each card.)* The Recent Past? The Moon: losing direction and purpose. The Present? The Hanged Man: giving up control. The Near Future? Ah ha. The Eight of Wands: moving to a conclusion, having a meaningful conversation.

*AARON takes out his cellphone.*

Here we go.

*He turns it on.*

*Light shift.*

**WILL**
*(on phone)* Hello, Awkward Moments Bistro. Table for two? Sure we can get you something at the back.

*Music: "Happy Ending."*

*WILL puts the phone away.*

Oooo that's going to be one uncomfortable lunch date. Or who knows maybe it'll be wonderful. Maybe Susan's always wanted a... a... a... One of those. Maybe everything will be a really truly and really and truly a happily ever after.

*Music: "Happy Ending."*

But the chances of that are slimmer than a crackhead on a fast. So where are we at now in terms of story? *(WILL goes to the table and pours a vodka.)* Let's see. Well Warren has decided to go and get his stuff. And that's a good thing. And in deciding to do that he's blown off a lunch meeting with Susan. So as a result Susan has rebooked a lunch date with her new "boy" friend Aaron. Which means that Aaron now can't look after her—his—her?—his?—whatever—nephew. And now the kid has to be babysat by his ne'er-do-well alcoholic father Mike. Whew. Gosh I hope nothing happens to the kid.

*WILL takes a big drink of vodka. A phone rings. Sound of bottles falling over. Light shift.*

**MIKE**

Is that my phone? No? Is that my phone? I thought that was my phone. No? I'm waiting on a call. No phone? No phone. No pool. No pets. *(He sings.)* "I ain't got no cigarettes"... *(re: vodka)* Don't worry about this. This is not a problem. This is not a problem. If I had a problem—and I've got lots of problems—but if I were going to say I had one problem I'd say my problem is I don't think I feel. I don't mean "I don't think, I feel." I mean I think instead of feel I mean. A normal person would just say "I think too much." Which makes me I guess not a normal person. Because I think too much. My kid he's a feeler. I'm trying to get him a little more into his head. He lives with his mother. Seven years old can't ride a bike. I was born riding a bike. Seven years old and he can't skate, can't swim, can't ride a bike. How's he ever going to escape? *(laughs)* But I made her get him a bike though. Some Saturdays I take him out on it with the training wheels. *(He considers the drink in his hand.)* It's all good it's all good. I'm not drinking like I used to. Not heavy like I did. I was not a social drinker. I was a pound-myself-over-the-head-with-the-bottle-till-I-blacked-out drinker. But now I'm more social. And now I've got the program. I go to meetings. Now and then. It's all good. I'm not saying I'm not drinking I'm just not drinking like I used to. Just I get lonely. Not dangerous lonely, regular lonely. "I'm so lonely" then have a drink, that kind of lonely. Not "I'm so lonely" then *(mimes hanging himself)*. And I think too much when I'm not drinking. When I'm not drinking I'm like a brain dragging a spine around. When I'm drinking I'm okay, I'm right in there, I'm not thinking, have a laugh, have a drink. But I still go to meetings anyway. You can go to meetings and drink. I mean you can't drink *at* the meetings. Yeah yeah, "Open bar over by the Big Books, by the lit-er-a-ture stand. Have a chip!" There are different kinds of meetings you can go to. I like what they call a "low bottom" meeting—a *low bottom* meeting—that's where

people tell stories about alcohol poisoning and meds and incar-
ceration. I'm not so much for the "high bottom" meetings—a
*high bottom* meeting—those meetings where the parking lot is
full of foreign cars and they're telling stories about going wild
at the office Christmas party or blacking out on their Mexican
holiday. Not my world. But no matter what meeting you go to
the principles are the same. The central principle being: main
thing is: you have to give over. Give it over. So I give over and
give over and give over and I give over and I give over and I Give
Over and I *give over! (He laughs.)* Mondays are fine. No desire to
drink on Mondays. Monday, Tuesday, Wednesday, not so bad.
Thursday I'm getting a little antsy. Friday I wake up scratching
my head wondering: "Why'd I stop?" Friday night I forget to even
wonder. Friday night is hard especially if I'm seeing the kid on
Saturday. Saturday's the day I'm sometimes supposed to see the
kid. It always helps if I'm a little hungover. I get in there then,
have a laugh with him. As long as I don't have a drink. If I don't
have a drink in the morning I know I'm all right. *(notes the drink
in his hand)* Yeah yeah yeah but yeah but. That's all right. See it
wasn't the plan to see him today. Yesterday it wasn't the plan.
I'm waiting on a call. I wouldn't have had a drink if I knew I was
seeing him today. If that was the plan. But it's all good. I just
go with the flow. Most Saturdays I never know what to do with
him. Sometimes I take him down to the library. I used to spend
a good deal of time in the library. I'm no big reader though. I
first started going for the free newspapers and because I was
trying to quit smoking. I met my wife at the library. Ex-wife.

His mother. She's a character. She's a big reader. Disappears into a book and calls it a holiday. Maybe that was my big mistake. She sees me at the library and thinks I'm some big kind of reader. A big reader and all that goes along with that. And not having all that came along with that not too much but shit came of that. No no that's not true. There was good stuff… There's the kid. He's still there. Saturdays. Or if not the library maybe a movie. But there's not too many movies he likes. Mostly he just wants to watch this one movie over and over and over. This cartoon about a princess mermaid. Which I think is a little… But he's just a kid. He likes science. And he likes science. I liked science. I see me in him some ways. Or forget the movie. I might take him to this Chinese restaurant I go to. I've been going there for years. They know me there. This angry Chinese waiter and I have this joke fight thing going. He's not really angry though he's just excited; he's not even Chinese he's Korean. I took my wife—ex-wife there for our very first date. Shrimp fried rice, moo goo gai pan and Peking chicken. Peeking chicken! Peeking chicken! Peekaboo peeking chicken! And then after they bring us the fortune cookies. And this is beautiful this is beautiful. After, they bring us— Wait back up back up back up. You gotta know this. Always always forever with me with fortune cookies I always go for the fortune cookie farthest away. And you're not supposed to do that right. You're supposed to take the cookie closest to you. The one closest to you is the one that God or the Universe or Buddha or whatever put your fortune in. But I always took the one farthest away because that way I had some say in my fortune. Like if God or the Universe or Buddha or whatever put that cookie close to me because it was supposed to be my fortune then I was going to trick them up and find my own fortune. I'd get to choose my destiny by taking the one farthest away. So this first night of the first date they bring out the fortune cookies and before I even make a move she goes for the one farthest away from her. She goes for the one by me farthest from her. And so I go for the one by her farthest from me. So hey, right, maybe we got one another's fortunes. But what's really beautiful? Really? She takes the cookie, doesn't open it, doesn't take it out of the wrapper or anything, and she drops it in her purse and she says, "I'm going to save this for later." Awwww. I saved mine too. I never said anything though. I've still got it. Not crushed up or anything. It's in a cigar box with my birth certificate and an old Bobby Orr Boston Bruins hockey card. I doubt she's still got hers though.

*He rubs his head like it hurts from thinking.*

But it's hard in the restaurant with the kid because there's not a lot of dads alone with their seven-year-old kids. I don't see them anyway. And I don't know what to say to him half the time and it's harder at the restaurant because I keep thinking people know, people can see I don't know what to say. "Oh that guy doesn't know what to say to his kid." Sometimes I think maybe I should be the clown and stick some chalkstips in my mouth and be like, "I am the Walrus!" But he'd just think that was stupid. Ah! Ah! See right there? See that? See why do I have to think that? Why do I have to think that. He's not going to think it's stupid he would think it was funny. See what happens when I think too much. I'm getting better though. I used to be real bad. Before I stopped heavy drinking. But now I'm good as long as I don't have a drink in the morning. *(He regards the glass in his hand.)* Yeah yeah but I'm okay, I'm okay. Ah it doesn't matter. A couple of times before I went over to pick him up on Saturday morning with a glow on and a bottle in my pocket, no big deal. He likes it. I mean he doesn't know I've been drinking but he thinks I'm funny. "You're funny." She won't care. She won't know. She won't lay eyes on me. She won't have me in the house. By *court order.* That was our house one time. Sleep in on Saturdays. He was a baby. Or before he was there. Stay in bed all day. Eat sandwiches. Crumbs in the sheets. Who cares? That part of her back. Softest place ever. *(He hits himself on the head; he laughs.)* I think too much! But you know what? If the plan is to see him today? If I get the call? Then I know what I'm going to do. Because she's always, "You made me buy him that goddamn bike but you won't take him out on it." But if the plan is I see him today then today is the day the training wheels come off. That's how you learn. Get right into it. That's what a father does. Get right up there with him, give him a good push, have a laugh. I'm not a good father.

What?

Oh, that's not fair. That's not fair. "I'm NOT a bad father." That's not fair. "Oh he said—hear what he said?" I don't care what you think. I don't care what you think. I don't care what she thinks. I don't care what anyone thinks. I care what he thinks though. I care what he thinks. Because I don't want him to have to grow up and some day be sitting there with his wife or his girlfriend and have to tell her: "My dad didn't even teach me how to ride a bike."

*MIKE knocks back the drink.*

**WILL**
Ahhh.

*The phone rings.*

*Light shift.*

And there's the call.

*Music: "Happy Ending."*

Hmm, that drink made me feel like... Another.

*WILL reaches under the table and takes out a vodka bottle and pours another drink.*

Oh I know, the poor guy. Some people just can't help being themselves. What it really comes down to is some people just can't handle their own lives so they need a little medication. One man's cocktail is another man's prescription. And why can't they handle it? Because they give their story away. They give it over. Look, in life, you can be a passenger or you can be a driver. If you want to get your stuff you have to drive. It's very simple. You want the girl? Get the girl. You want to know your fortune? Open the cookie. You want to tell the story? Go and get your stuff. And hey, is that what we're supposed to be doing? What are we doing sitting around here? Let's go get our stuff. But we could wait around for a minute or two. That way you'd get to meet the kid. Before we kill him.

*Light shift and giant music, Marilyn Manson's "This Is The New Shit."*

*KEVIN does his giant dance.*

**KEVIN**

Once upon a time there was this guy. Heeee was this guy. Heeee was just this guuuuy. Just this guy with a wife and two kids: one kid a twin boy and one kid a twin girl. And every night they'd all have dinner of pizza that he picked up in his car for takeout on his way home from work where he worked as aaaaaaaa dentist! And he was a dentist because he had really clean hands and really really fresh breath and these glasses things you could wear to watch movies in the chair and it made it looked like the movies were on the ceiling but they weren't on the ceiling they were just in the glasses things—*It's Ariel and her beautiful hair and flow-ing red and beautiful in the swimming of underwater: "I am Ariel"*—and not on the ceiling but just right there in the glasses things right in front of your eyes. So there's this guy who was a dentist and his wife was his wife and his two kids who were two kids, one kid a twin boy and one twin a twin girl, and everyone was really happy but not really. And because everyone was really happy but not really, every night the guy would go into the basement and drink magic juice. The magic juice was magic because it made the guy feel a little bit better and a little bit funny and a little bit bigger. The magic juice was also poison but it was only poison if you drank too much. But because it made the guy feel a little bit better and a little bit funny and little bit bigger, every night he drank just a little bit too much. And one night there was a terrible fight about pizza. Because they had pizza every night. And every night was too much of pizza for the guy's wife and one night she just starting yelling and crying: "I'M SO SICK OF THIS. I'M JUST SO SICK OF THIS. I DON'T LOVE PIZZA. I NEVER LOVED PIZZA. I'M JUST SO SICK OF THIS." And the guy got really mad and almost crying too: "YOU'RE TELLING ME NOW! YOU'RE TELLING ME NOW! WHY DIDN'T YOU TELL ME BEFORE? WHY ARE YOU TELLING ME NOW!" And that night the guy goes into the basement and he's so upset and he drinks all of the magic juice. Every single drop from every single bottle. Even drops from bottles all sticky like they've been there since last summer even bottles with cigarette butts in them. Then everyone goes to bed. And everything gets very very very very very very very very

very very quiet. Then everybody wakes up and it's morning and the guy brushes his teeth and drinks his coffee—not at the same time! And the guy goes to put on his shoes but his shoes don't fit. They are just a little too tight. So the guy goes and gets these other shoes he got for Christmas that were just a little too big but now they fit just perfect. And so he goes to work and it's a normal day. "Good morning, Miss Green, you look very pretty today what are my appointments? Hello, Mister Babbledob, how are your teeth today? Are you flossing and brushing after every meal, Jeanie? Good afternoon, little boy, would you like to watch a movie on my special glasses? What a long day I'm very tired good night, Miss Green." And then the guy goes home and even still gets pizza like normal because he just wants everything to be normal and he doesn't know what else to do but pizza because pizza is normal. And then he goes to bed. Then the next morning the guy wakes up and he goes to put on his pants but his pants don't fit so he makes his belt bigger and thinks, "No more pizza for me!" And then the next morning he wakes up and he goes to work and his head keeps hitting the ceiling of his car so he has to drive like this bent over. And the next day he goes to work and his fingers are too big to fit in anybody's mouth. And so he has to take a vacation, but he takes the kind of vacation where he just stays in his bedroom and won't come out. But in his bedroom he keeps getting bigger and bigger and bigger until he busts through the walls of the house. But not a fast bust-through like an explosion bust-through, but a minute by minute slow bust-through where it's "wood creak creak creak wood, snap" and "wood creak creak creak wood, snap" and then the walls of the bedroom are on the ground and it's the guy who's holding up the house and they have to go and get these strong guys who come with these metal poles with holes in it that you screw up really slow and heavy—up and up and up and up—to hold up the whole house so the guy can come out. And he comes out and now he's a giant. And because he's a giant he has to go away. And there are feelings. The wife and her feelings but "I don't want to talk about it" but they were maybe going to get a divorce about pizza anyway. And maybe she should have told him before. And the kids have their feelings, some sad and some not. Some not like "it's quiet because nobody's yelling and knocking stuff down" and some sad like "who's going to help me do my science homework" and "who's going to take me out for Halloween as the Little Mermaid"—that was the girl twin who had that feeling. But he doesn't know where to go so for a while he lives all alone out in the woods past the swamp behind the soccer field by the school where nobody hardly ever goes just the bad kids who do drugs and make sex on those girls from the other high school. But the guy keeps getting bigger and bigger and bigger and all the people of the whole town are all like, "What the hell, you're blocking out all the sun from the whole town, get the hell out of here." So he has to go away. And so he walks and walks and walks and he has to be very very careful where he walks because he's not just a Jack in the Beanstalk kind of giant but he's like a mountain kind of giant with airplanes in his hair and clouds are all in his eyes, with just one step he could crush a whole neighbourhood. So he walks very very slowly, very very carefully, until he gets to a place where all the giants hang out. Which is a bar. And in the bar there's a TV where there is only one show on all the time. Which is *Cheers*. So that you're watching a show in a bar of a bar—in a bar of a bar—in a bar of a bar. And because then whenever anybody walks in and says: "What's on?" Everybody gets to go: *Cheers*. Cheers! Glug glug glug glug. And the giants are always standing around saying how good it is the little people aren't around anymore. And the giant guy is like: "Yeah me too!" But that's not true. No no that's not true. Because some nights he called home—but it was hard to hear him on the phone because he has a giant voice and it's just a regular phone and he was maybe crying. And once he came back in person and broke the door and the giant cops had to come put a coudorer... a coradora...... a courtordera on him. "Okay, people, nothing to see here move along, move along, y'all go back to your happy homes." And the giant guy he's crying and crying all the time now and then one day he stops crying long enough to go and wash his face. But the only place he can wash his face is the ocean, so he goes to the ocean and he leans over it and he sees his reflection and in his reflection he sees there's something in his forehead. It's a door. He never noticed that before, he thought that bump was just a pimple but it's not it's a doorknob. So he opens the door and in his head is this teeny tiny guy. And the giant guy says to the teeny tiny guy, "What the hell are you doing in there?" And the teeny tiny guy jumps out onto the giant guy's shoulder and the giant says, "What the hell is your name?" And the teeny tiny guy says, "I am Will." And then the giant guy gets it. He gets it. He gets it he gets it he gets it. This is the teeny tiny guy who has been living in his head from since way from before. Telling him all the wrong things to do. Telling him to drink the magic juice, telling him to get pizza only and never think of something new, telling him to only be grumpy and never give hugs, to go into his room and not come out, telling him not to believe in God. No giants believe in God. Uh uh, uh uh, uh uh. Because they don't believe the angels are strong enough to carry their giant prayers to heaven. But all they'd have to do is ask for more angels. The angels should know that too but angels aren't angels because they're smart. And now the giant is mad because he knows it is Will who made him a giant. So he goes to grab Will but Will jumps off his shoulder and down to the ground and runs away. So the giant starts running after Will because he thinks if he can catch him and crush him that everything will go back to normal and he won't be a giant anymore. So the giant starts running and as he runs he stomps. Stomping and stomping and stomping. And even still today. And every time he stomps that's why there's earthquakes, and the giant is yelling and that's why there's thunder, and the giant is crying and every time a teardrop hits the ground that's why there's floods, and the giant is swooshing his arms to try and grab Will and that's why there's tornadoes. *(whispering)* So be very very very careful if you hear a voice telling you to do things you know you shouldn't do

because you might turn into a giant too. *(a long pause as* KEVIN *regards the audience passively)*
I made that up.

But it's true.

Today my dad's maybe going to teach me how to ride a bike without training wheels.

If he ever calls.

*The phone rings.*

KEVIN *is excited.*

**WILL**
Oh shut the fuck up.

*Light shift.*

*Music: "Happy Ending."*

Well I've been described a lot of ways in the past but never as "a teeny tiny guy." I don't think so. I'm bigger than all of you. Listen to... *(re: music)*

Okay I think we've made our point with that.

I said I think I've made my point.

WILL *gestures sharply. Record scratching. Music ends.*

Listen to the teeny tiny guy. Tell your story, Warren. Go and get your stuff.

**WARREN**

I'm walking. I'm walking. I'm walking. Around the corner. Past the market. A man in a green suit, a golden retriever at his side, a net bag hangs from his arm, inside the bag is a bottle of wine. I'm walking. I'm walking. The pastry shop. The liquor store. A woman in a tailored coat and polished shoes passes carrying a case of imported lager, a younger woman walks beside her whining—the woman snaps "shut up." I'm standing in front of the smoke shop. I've quit but I go inside. Time passes and I'm opening a pack of cigarettes as I cross the street. An angry taxi driver. An old dog. I get a light from a crazy man who smells like something sweet. In a window over the bookstore across the street three blond men with bare chests toast one another with glasses of something clear. Passing the Italian bistro. My car keys are in my hand. On the patio a couple talk seriously. He is in a blue cap; he drinks beer, tall, cold just poured. She is in a high-necked sweater and brown pants; she's not drinking; she picks at the skin on the back of her hands. He leans across the table to make a point and knocks over his glass. The beer runs across the table and pools at the edge dripping onto her brown pants. Drip drip drip drip drip. But she doesn't react. And as I pass she looks up at me. And her eyes are full. Her eyes are full of everything. Then a blank spot. And I'm in a bar. And a blank spot. And a third shot. And a blank spot. And I'm in my car. I'm driving but I don't want to be. Yes yes I do want to be! I do want to be! I want to get my stuff. I want my windbreaker and my sneakers and that book and my tax stuff and my John Denver CD. Why didn't he know I liked John Denver? He didn't even care enough to know. John Denver left his wife. His first wife Annie. He wrote that song for her. He was sorry he left. His second wife got his name.

**VOICE OF WILL**

That's right, Warren. The second wife turned out to be quite a cunt.

**WARREN**

Don't say that! That's not nice, that's not nice. But that's not him. He's not like that. That's not you. I just make you sound that way because I'm afraid. I'm afraid I won't see you again. I just want to hear you laugh. I just want to see you smile. He used to do this happy dance. I want to see the happy dance.

**VOICE OF WILL**

That bastard wasn't smiling he was laughing at you.

**WARREN**

I'm driving fast. I take the hill hard. I think I lose a hubcap but I don't even look back to see if it's on the road. I'm headed down the hill toward the school. The soccer field. It must be Saturday because the soccer field is empty. I used to play soccer there. I hated playing soccer. The house is just two lefts and a right from here. That big house. That pool I paid for. Empty schoolyard. Chain-link fence. Keep my eyes on the road.

**VOICE OF WILL**

Is he happy now? Is he happy now?

**WARREN**

Bike wheel spinning. Bike wheel spinning. Little boy's face. Little boy's face. He's learning how to ride. His dad runs beside him. Gives him a push. Bike wheel spinning. Little boy's face. You never took care of me. Why didn't you take care of me? Did you expect me to ask? I couldn't ask. I just wanted you to know. Keep my eyes on the road.

**VOICE OF WILL**

Why didn't he take care of you?

**WARREN**

Bike wheel spinning. Bike wheel spinning. Little boy's face. Little boy's face. I just want to hear you laugh. I just want to see you smile. I just want a happy ending. Why can't I have a happy ending?

**VOICE OF WILL**

Because you're not fucking good enough!

*Light and sound shift.*

**WARREN**

Through the air the bike careening little boy his arms and legs flapping wildly trapped in flight, rebounds off the windshield, windshield shatters fast like frost, spin the wheel the car is turning deep into the soccer field, time is moving in slow motion, little boy flies high and far like sleeping dancing, meets the craggy tar. Bouncing like an empty jug. Bike wheel spinning bike wheel spinning bike wheel spinning bike wheel spinning.

*Light shift.*

**WILL**

Now there's an ending. Very dramatic. The kid dies. And Warren kills him.

And Mike he has to be held responsible too. He's the dad, had a few drinks, gives the kid a push.

And good old Uncle Aaron. If Uncle Aaron hadn't been so hot for Susan the kid wouldn't have ended up with Mike.

And Susan, if Susan had been a little less demanding, a little gentler, then Warren wouldn't have ended up behind the wheel.

So many lives destroyed.

And for what?

For a story.

For you.

What? You were expecting a happy ending. Well it's just one kid. It could have been worse. It could have been quadruplets. That would have been four times worse! Or he could have T-boned a bus full of children. Or driven into a hospital of sick kids and blown it up. Or been manning a satellite that hits an island of infants—or imploded a planet of teenagers. You want a happy ending? What did you ever do to deserve a happy ending? You want a happy ending go home and watch TV. Or go shopping. Welcome to Walmart, maggots. I am will and I get what I want and I don't care how. You got a problem with that?

> *Through the preceding giant stomping has been growing closer. Now the stomping is upon us. WILL looks up.*

Holy shit!

> *Blackout and the sound of bones snapping and flesh compressing.*

> *Light up.*

**KEVIN**
"Holy shit!" are Will's last words before the twin boy steps on him and squishes him.

Because Will is not only teeny tiny to a giant he is a teeny tiny guy even to a kid. And the rule is that if a kid sees Will and steps on him then time goes backward and everything goes into revere and everything turns into a happy ending.

*KEVIN becomes ME.*

I just made that up.

*Light shift. As ME speaks to us he dresses in his street clothes.*

**ME**

Nobody dies. No. Warren doesn't go to the barbecue. Instead he answers his phone and ends up going out to lunch with his lawyer Susan. He does go on a nasty bender though. And Aaron the astrologer thinks about the tarot reading he did and realizes that it was less about Susan and more about his ex-girlfriend and Aaron realized he has a lot of work to do on his feelings about his ex-girlfriend. And Susan starts spending more time with her daughters. The older one does end up going to prison but just for a year and a half. While she's in prison she learns how to sew. When she gets out she opens a dress shop and she becomes more famous than Vera Wang. And Susan and her younger daughter go on a vacation to Costa Rica and they have a pretty good time. There are even some pictures of the daughter smiling and wearing shorts which Susan thinks is a very good sign. Oh right, some people do die. Gervase and Sonja the models die. They end up dying in a fire at their old place. But at least they're together.

But the turtle survives the fire though, and she ends up living to be twenty-six. And the world doesn't end in five years or eight years. But everything does change. And Mike's ex-wife actually did save her fortune cookie. And Mike starts going to his meetings regularly and stops drinking all together and his ex-wife lets him move back in and this makes Kevin very happy. And one night Mike and his wife are alone and they light some candles and they open up their fortune cookies together and they both have the same fortune: "You will fall in love." And pink becomes the new black for real. And the Little Mermaid gets an eternal soul and lives in heaven with God forever. And Arthur Schopenhauer ends up becoming famous at the age of seventy and learns how play the fiddle. And one night Warren goes to a twelve-step meeting and he's in really rough shape and after the meeting this guy comes up and talks to him and Warren and the guy end up going for coffee. And Warren and the guy talk for hours and the guy ends up becoming Warren's sponsor. And the guy turns out to be Mike. And Mike and Warren become really good friends.

*ME is now standing dressed to leave, holding his Starbucks coffee.*

Oh, and one more thing. One day Warren has a package arrive at his apartment delivered by a courier company. And it's a box, and in the box are his windbreaker and his sneakers and a John Denver CD...

*John Denver's "Annie's Song" begins to play quietly. ME listens
for a moment.*

Cue the snow.

*Presently it begins to snow.*

It's not the same John Denver CD but it has all the same songs.
And in the box is his tax stuff that he doesn't end up really need-
ing anyway. And three books, the book he wanted, his favourite
novel that he'd forgotten about and a book called *Lick the Sugar
Habit* that he keeps meaning to read. And in the box is a cap that
Warren doesn't recognize but it fits him like a glove and it does
look rather jaunty. And at the bottom of the box is a note. And
the note says: "I'm sorry how it ended."

*It continues to snow as the light fades.*

*End.*

## ACKNOWLEDGEMENTS

The playwright wishes to thank Necessary Angel Theatre Company, Matt White, Guy de Carteret, Rob Harding, Marcie Januska, LouAnn Chiasson, Karl Blindheim, Gerard MacIssac, and the members of the wedding.

© Guntar Kravis

Daniel MacIvor is one of Canada's most accomplished play-wrights and performers. Winner of the prestigious Elinore and Lou Siminovitch Prize, the GLAAD Award, the Governor General's Literary Award, and many others, Daniel's plays have been met with acclaim throughout North America.

First edition: April 2014

Printed and bound in Canada by General Printers, Oshawa

Cover photo © Guntar Kravis

Cover and book design by Blake Sproule

**PLAYWRIGHTS CANADA PRESS**

202-269 Richmond St. W.

Toronto, ON

M5V 1X1

416.703.0013

info@playwrightscanada.com

www.playwrightscanada.com

MIX
Paper from
responsible sources
FSC® C023656